Moments
Matter

Everyday Inspiration from a Soulful CEO

John B. Goodman

JBG
Chaska, MN

Published by
John B. Goodman
c/o The Goodman Group
1107 Hazeltine Boulevard, Suite 200
Chaska, MN 55318

Publisher's Cataloging-in-Publication Data
Goodman, John B.

>Moments matter : everyday inspiration from a soulful CEO / John B. Goodman. – Chaska, MN : John B. Goodman, 2015.

>p. ; cm.

>ISBN13: 978-0-9980001-4-5

>1. Businessmen—Conduct of life. 2. Success. 3. Self-realization. I. Title.

>HF5386.G66 2015

>650.1—dc23   2015906369

Project coordination by Jenkins Group, Inc.,
www.BookPublishing.com

Creative Director, Yvonne Fetig Roehler

Interior and cover design by Brooke Camfield

Printed in the United States of America
19 18 17 16 15 • 5 4 3 2 1

This book is dedicated to you.
May you always know your Greatness.

Moments Matter was created to help inspire and encourage you in every aspect of your life.

Whatever you're experiencing at any given moment—whether it's issues with work, relationships, health, or family—these thoughts can help you see things in a new light.

Keep *Moments Matter* on your desk or nightstand and turn to any page whenever you need inspiration.

I hope you will find the peace and joy you are meant to experience.

If you believe it, you can be it. Believing that you can do something is your first step toward accomplishing it.

There comes a time to let go and rewrite the script. Sometimes that isn't easy because hanging on to the familiar seems safer than venturing into the unknown.

Once you let your ego take a backseat to what your heart says is right, you'll experience tremendous learning and growth.

We can't necessarily change events, but we can certainly change how we respond to them.

Before a trapeze artist can grab the second trapeze, he or she must let go of the first. Before we can move forward, we have to let go of the past. That moment of letting go is terrifying, but we need to have faith.

If you want certain qualities in a relationship, you must first exhibit those qualities in yourself.

There are no limits in life except those we choose to put upon ourselves.

The universe continually gives us opportunities. It's our responsibility to learn from our mistakes and challenges so when we face a similar situation, we can choose a better path.

Joy comes from within.

If we're always in pursuit of the elusive dream, we might never see or realize what we're accomplishing in the moment.

You can succeed at any moment, in any place, when you're willing to let go of the past, the desire for control, and the notion that everything must be done the way you've always done it.

They say intuition is God talking to us through our thoughts.

In frailty and vulnerability,
we shine.

Change may come
through force or out of choice,
but it will happen.

The best thing that any of us can do is meditate, get centered, and recognize our connectedness with the higher spirit that resides in all of us.

It's amazing how the universe turns up the volume. If we don't get the message the first time, it will reappear in a different form and at a higher volume.

Make a change and let that change radiate. Others will make changes, and eventually change will be the norm, not the exception.

Everything is energy.

Life is like a curved road.
If we concentrate on what's
taking place at the moment and
negotiate the present situation,
we can come through any
experience safely.

Love is eternal and can never be taken away, lost, or terminated.

Once we give up the fear of death, the fear of our ultimate loss of control and of nothingness, then we can get on with living.

Life is a classroom. Sometimes you don't have the answers, and you must discover what you still need to learn.

Detachment works well. You can appreciate things for what they are and not get hooked by the drama.

If you want everyone around you to change, then you need to change yourself first.

We must come home to ourselves, accept ourselves as being enough, and get in touch with that God-like energy in each of us.

If you can come up with alternative explanations for what's happening, you can gain more insight into human nature and have more compassion for others and yourself.

Every day is a new day, every dawn a new beginning. So try something different.

It is important to release
attachment to all that we aren't,
all that we don't have, and all that
we wish we could be. We need
to recognize our divinity and the
beauty of our existence.

Life is about feeling. If we get out of our heads and move into our hearts, we can respond not from how we think, but from how we feel.

Everything in life helps us evolve.
We can learn through joy and sorrow.

The more you honor your soul's temple—the body—the clearer you become, the more energy you have, and the more you become centered and living in the moment.

The reward of an experience far outweighs the fear of it.

Do something because you love it, not for approval. Do it for no other reason than simple joy.

Look to find the balance
between doing and being.

It's important to follow your gut instinct even when you can't pinpoint why.

Take a long-term view of life.
Don't focus only on what's
expedient for today or tomorrow.

Unfamiliarity or discomfort
is necessary to introduce us
to new behaviors, new thoughts,
and new belief systems.

If we can become in tune with the universe and with the natural flow of energies, then we can start making decisions from that power source within us. We can learn how to be strong in our convictions, knowing that our inner knowledge rings true and is there to guide and to support us.

We have all the answers we will ever need within us, and our responsibility is to learn how to access those answers.

If we hang on to anger
and insist on righteousness,
we lock that energy inside
and it can't flow freely.

In opening up, we can learn the
possibilities of being nurtured
and learn to receive.

Life is a mirror; we will attract whatever we are.

A desire to live more joyfully
is reason enough to be
forgiving of others.

The key is not getting attached to the outcome, but knowing that when you're one with God, the outcome will always be what it's supposed to be.

Love is why we are here.

We must stop thinking about tomorrow's work or yesterday's missed opportunities and be present like no other moment exists.

If you see life from the outside in, practice seeing the world from the inside out.

Our psyche can change if we nurture ourselves in a positive, loving way through nutrition and our thoughts.

A compliment is just the flip side of criticism; the challenge is not to be moved by either.

If we are able to break the chains and heal the wounds, our problems won't get passed down to our children.

Trust that life is unfolding just as it is meant to at any given moment.

Recognize that you don't know
all the answers and don't need
to control everything at every
moment. Leave room for the
magical and mystical universe
to help support you.

With a new day can come a new feeling of excitement and exuberance if you believe it.

Be present in the moment and see the difference it makes in your ability to be there for somebody, to listen, to be connected.
Being present without thinking of the future or dwelling on the past is a wonderful gift.

Picture death like the sunrise and the sunset; it's just another transition. We will be here for as long as it takes us to learn whatever we need to learn, or do whatever we need to do, and then we'll choose to move on to the next experience.

Do the inner work on yourself.
Be it. Love it. Don't just speak it.

About the Author

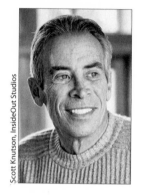

Scott Knutson, InsideOut Studios

John B. Goodman, Chairman of The Goodman Group, has spent 45 years building a family property management company into an award-winning organization that creates and manages living environments that emphasize quality of life. He attributes his success to a holistic approach, one that recognizes the whole individual; body, mind, and spirit. The Goodman Group's innovative programs bring to life quality conscious/value oriented principles, and enable residents and staff to achieve an optimum level of wellbeing.

John has been a featured speaker at the Massachusetts Institute of Technology, the National Association of Senior Living Industries, and the University of Minnesota Carlson School of Management. He is committed to providing leadership that fosters personal growth and achievement, along with creating ways in which business can play a positive role in society.

He is the recipient of the 2002 Ellis Island Medal of Honor and in 2011 was named Citizen of the Year by Florida's Largo Mid-Pinellas Chamber of Commerce. In 2015, The Goodman Group proudly received the Performance Excellence Award-Advancement level in accordance with the national Malcolm Baldrige Criteria for Performance Excellence.

John B. Goodman is also the author of *The Road to Self, Reflections from a Soulful CEO.*

To learn more about The Goodman Group visit
www.thegoodmangroup.com

Notes

Notes